Through the Night

by

Donna Rose Porta Kochner

Illustrated by

Nancy Cote

WestBow Press books may be ordered through booksellers or by contacting:

WestBow Press
A Division of Thomas Nelson & Zondervan
1663 Liberty Drive
Bloomington, IN 47403
www.westbowpress.com
844-714-3454

Because of the dynamic nature of the Internet, any web addresses or links contained in this book may have changed since publication and may no longer be valid. The views expressed in this work are solely those of the author and do not necessarily reflect the views of the publisher, and the publisher hereby disclaims any responsibility for them.

Any people depicted in stock imagery provided by Getty Images are models, and such images are being used for illustrative purposes only. Certain stock imagery © Getty Images.

ISBN: 978-1-4497-6999-4 (sc)
ISBN: 978-1-4497-7000-6 (e)

Library of Congress Control Number: 2012918673

Print information available on the last page.

WestBow Press rev. date: 02/01/2022

WESTBOW
PRESS®
A DIVISION OF THOMAS NELSON
& ZONDERVAN

Dedicated to my grandchildren:
Lexy, Elliott, Kaden, Daniel, Ashlynne Rose,
Daven, Annalye, Beniah, Andi Grace, Estella,
and those to come
With love, always, and forever,
Grandma   D.R.P.K.

To Harper and Liam love N.C.

When I awake through the night
In my mind I hug and hold you tight.

I picture you asleep in bed
The covers tucked around your head.

The peace I see upon your face
Tells me you're in another place.

Resting safely while you dream
Of heart desires yet unseen.

Though in reality we're far apart
I hold you gently in my heart.

Knowing the Lord is with us both
Helps me feel you're actually close.

So if in your dreams you feel a tug

It's Jesus giving you my hug.

Sleep tight,
Love, Grandma

Printed in the United States
by Baker & Taylor Publisher Services